Wild and pet puppies

Bobbie Kalman

Crabtree Publishing Company
www.crabtreebooks.com

It's fun to learn about **Baby Animals**

Created by Bobbie Kalman

For Pam Crossley and Whiskey, her wild puppy!

**Author and
Editor-in-Chief**
Bobbie Kalman

Editor
Kathy Middleton

Proofreader
Crystal Sikkens

Photo research
Bobbie Kalman
Crystal Sikkens

Design
Bobbie Kalman
Katherine Berti
Samantha Crabtree
    (logo and front cover)

Production coordinator
Katherine Berti

Illustrations
Barbara Bedell: pages 8, 10, 13
Margaret Amy Salter: pages 19, 24

Photographs
© BigStockPhoto.com: back cover, pages 15 (top), 17 (top and
    bottom left), 23 (bottom right), 24 (homes and wolves)
© Marc Crabtree: page 21 (middle right)
© Dreamstime.com: pages 5 (bottom), 7 (bottom left), 8,
    21 (bottom right), 22 (left), 24 (bodies)
© Shutterstock.com: front cover, pages 1, 5 (top), 6, 7 (top and
    bottom right), 9 (bottom), 10, 11, 12, 13 (all except top right),
    14, 15 (bottom), 16, 17 (background and bottom right), 18,
    20, 21 (top, middle left, and bottom left), 22 (right),
    23 (top and bottom left), 24 (dingos, food, foxes, jackals,
    and pet puppies)
Other images by Corel, Creatas, Digital Vision, and Photodisc

Library and Archives Canada Cataloguing in Publication

Kalman, Bobbie, 1947-
    Wild and pet puppies / Bobbie Kalman.

(It's fun to learn about baby animals)
Includes index.
ISBN 978-0-7787-3957-9 (bound).--ISBN 978-0-7787-3976-0 (pbk.)

    1. Canidae--Infancy--Juvenile literature. 2. Wild dogs--Infancy--
Juvenile literature. 3. Puppies--Juvenile literature. I. Title. II. Series.

QL737.C22K35 2008   j599.77'139   C2008-907018-6

Library of Congress Cataloging-in-Publication Data

Kalman, Bobbie.
  Wild and pet puppies / Bobbie Kalman.
      p. cm. -- (It's fun to learn about baby animals)
  Includes index.
  ISBN 978-0-7787-3976-0 (pbk. : alk. paper) -- ISBN 978-0-7787-3957-9
(reinforced library binding : alk. paper)
  1. Canidae--Infancy--Juvenile literature. 2. Puppies--Juvenile literature. I.
Title. II. Series.

  QL737.C22K364 2009
  599.77'137--dc22

                                                              2008046253

Crabtree Publishing Company

www.crabtreebooks.com   1-800-387-7650

**Published in Canada
Crabtree Publishing**
616 Welland Ave.
St. Catharines, Ontario
L2M 5V6

**Published in the United States
Crabtree Publishing**
PMB16A
350 Fifth Ave., Suite 3308
New York, NY 10118

**Published in the United Kingdom
Crabtree Publishing**
White Cross Mills
High Town, Lancaster
LA1 4XS

**Published in Australia
Crabtree Publishing**
386 Mt. Alexander Rd.
Ascot Vale (Melbourne)
VIC 3032

What is in this book?

What is a dog?

A dog is an animal called a **mammal**. Mammals have hair or fur on their bodies. Mammals are **born**. They come out of their mothers' bodies. **Pet dogs** live with people. **Wild dogs** do not live with people. Their homes are in **nature**. Nature is outdoor places not made by people.

Dogs have hair or fur on their bodies. Dogs are born.

This coyote pup is a wild dog. It lives in nature. The coyote pup lives on a mountain.

This fox mother is feeding her babies milk from her body.

Mammal mothers feed their babies milk. The milk is made in the bodies of mothers. Drinking mother's milk is called **nursing**. Both wild and pet puppies nurse from their mothers. These pet retriever pups are nursing.

Wild pups

Wolves, foxes, coyotes, African wild dogs, jackals, and dingos are wild dogs. Wild dogs live in different parts of the world. The babies of wild dogs are called pups or cubs.

fox

These dingo pups live in Australia.

These baby fox pups are red foxes. Red foxes live in many parts of the world.

Red foxes are not always red.
This red fox pup is black!

These African wild pups live
in grassy areas in Africa.

Wolves and coyotes

red wolf

There are gray wolves and red wolves. Gray wolves live in many places in the world. They live in the United States and Canada, too. There are very few red wolves left in the world!

gray wolves

This coyote pup is taking a drink of water. It lives in a forest in North America.

Coyotes live only in North America. They are cousins of wolves, but they are smaller than wolves. Jackals are like coyotes, but they live in other places. This jackal pup lives in Africa. Jackals eat birds, mice, and other small animals, just as coyotes do.

jackal pup

Pet puppies

All pet dogs belong to one dog group, but they do not all look the same. Some pet dogs are small, and others are really big. The biggest dog is the Irish wolfhound. Great Danes are almost as big. The smallest dog is the chihuahua. Baby pet dogs are called puppies.

Irish wolfhound

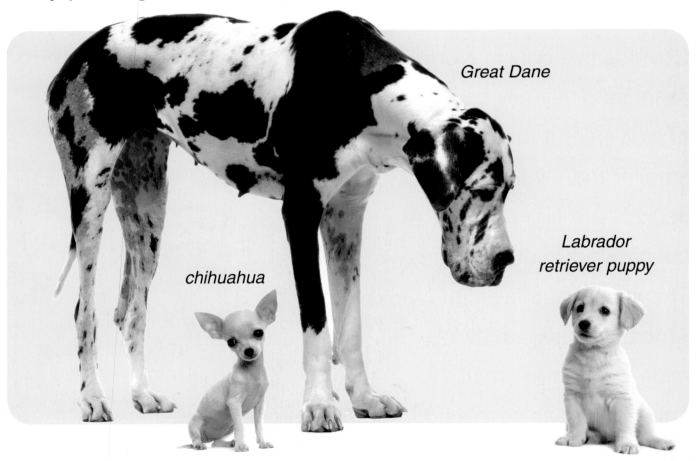

Great Dane

chihuahua

Labrador retriever puppy

Yorkshire terrier

beagle

Shar Pei puppies

Do you have a dog or puppy?
What kind is it? How many
kinds of dogs can you name?

Pomeranian

English bulldog

German
shepherd

Pet dogs
are part
of families.

pug puppy

Dog bodies

A dog's body is covered with fur or hair. Dogs have different kinds and colors of fur. Some fur is long and thick, and other fur is very short. This beagle puppy has short fur.

Dogs can see and hear very well.

*The nose and mouth of a dog are on its **snout**.*

A dog has a tail.

Dogs can find things with their strong sense of smell.

Dogs have four claws on each paw. They dig and scratch with their paws.

paw   *claws*

Dogs walk on four legs. Most dogs can run fast.

Dogs are **vertebrates**. Vertebrates are animals with **backbones**. Dogs have strong bodies with many bones inside. All the bones make up the **skeleton**.

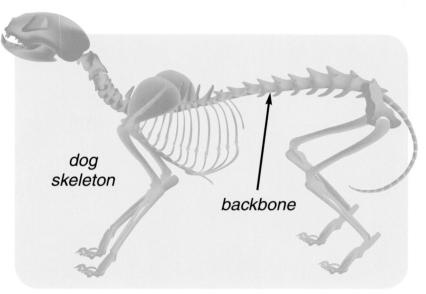

dog skeleton

backbone

This Chinese crested dog has some hair, but it has no fur.

This red fox is covered with thick fur.

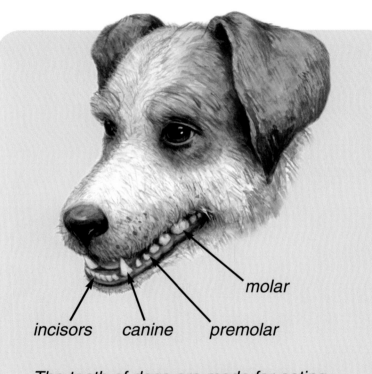

molar

incisors   canine   premolar

*The teeth of dogs are made for eating meat. A dog uses its **incisors**, or front teeth, for biting. Its **canines** are its fangs. Fangs are for tearing. The **premolars** and **molars** are for chewing food.*

13

What do pups eat?

Dogs are **carnivores**. Carnivores eat meat. After they are born, all puppies drink milk. They also start eating meat when they are a few weeks old.

A jackal mother is bringing up food from her stomach to feed to her pups. This food is liquid and is easy for the pups to eat.

Some dogs are **omnivores**. Omnivores eat more than one kind of food. Foxes are omnivores. They eat meat as well as plant foods such as fruit, leaves, and flowers. Jackals hunt other animals, but they are also **scavengers**. Scavengers eat dead animals killed by other carnivores.

This red fox pup has hunted its first meal with its mother's help. Soon it will hunt alone. The fox pup will also eat plants when it cannot find animals to eat.

These jackal pups are eating the leftovers of an animal that some lions have killed.

The homes of dogs

The natural places where animals live are called **habitats**. Some wild dogs find homes in the habitats where they live. Homes can be dead logs, caves, or **burrows**. Burrows are holes in the ground. Most pet dogs live in people's homes.

*This fox pup's home is a dead tree log. Its habitat is a **meadow**. A meadow is a field of grass.*

This small cave is the home of many coyote pups. Coyotes live in many kinds of habitats.

These wolves live in a burrow in a **forest** *habitat. Forests have many trees.*

Deserts *are dry places. These foxes live in a hot desert. A burrow is their home.*

What is a life cycle?

Dogs are born in **litters**. Litters are two or more pups. The pups grow and change. They become **adults**. Adults are fully grown dogs. Adult dogs can make babies of their own. Each time a new baby is born, a new **life cycle** begins. A life cycle is the set of changes in an animal from the time it is a baby to the time it becomes an adult.

a litter of newborn puppies

The life cycle of a wolf

These pictures show the life cycle of a wolf.

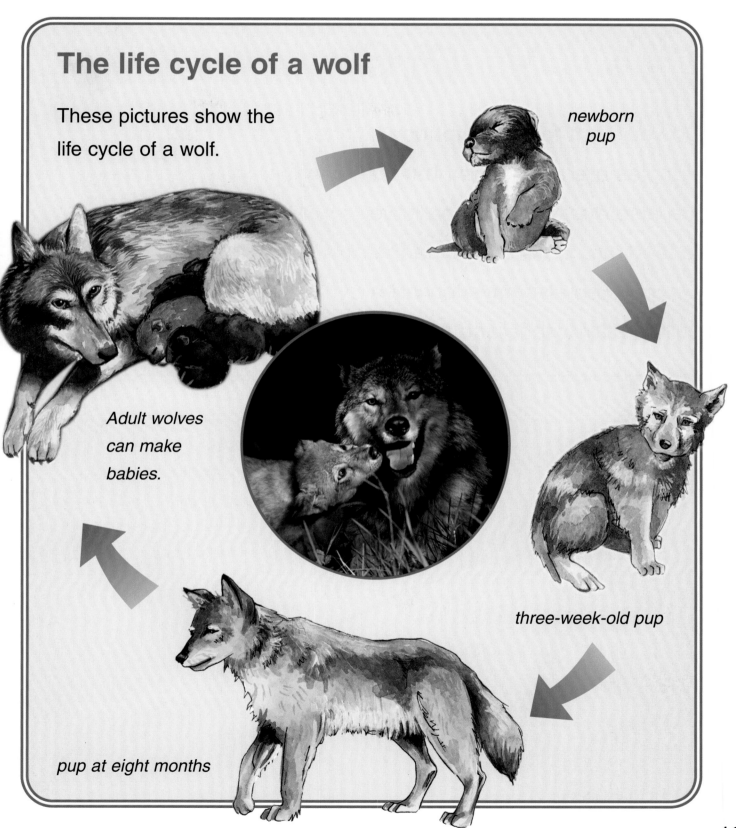

newborn pup

Adult wolves can make babies.

three-week-old pup

pup at eight months

19

Puppy love

Do you want to have a puppy? Puppies are a lot of fun, but they are also a lot of work. You have to feed and **groom**, or clean, a puppy. You also have to walk a puppy, play with it, and train it.

You need to take your puppy for a walk at least once a day. Some puppies are very strong, so you have to hold on tight to the leash! Do you walk your puppy, or does it walk you?

Puppies love to chew! Give them toy bones to chew on.

Puppies also need plenty of fresh water to drink!

You need to feed your puppy three to four times a day. Ask your **veterinarian** which puppy food is the best for your dog. A veterinarian is an animal doctor.

These brushes will help you groom your dog. You need to brush your dog every two days.

In summer, you can bathe your dogs outdoors.

Sending messages

Dogs send messages to other dogs and people to let them know how they are feeling. They use sounds and body language to **communicate**, or let others know what they want.

When a dog's ears are up, it is paying attention.

*This fox pup is showing love by **nipping** at its mother's mouth. Nipping is biting gently.*

A happy dog wags its tail.

The top wolf shows that he is the boss! The other wolf shows that he is afraid of him.

This wolf is baring its teeth and staring at an enemy. It is ready to fight!

One of these wolf cubs is crying for Mom!

Words to Know and Index

bodies
pages 4, 5, 12–13

coyotes
pages 4, 6, 8, 9, 17

dingos
page 6

food
pages 9, 13,
14–15, 21

foxes
pages 5, 6,
7, 13, 15,
16, 17, 22

homes
pages 16–17

jackals
pages 6,
9, 14, 15

life cycle
pages 18–19

pet puppies
pages 4, 5,
10–11, 12,
16, 20–21

wolves
pages 6, 8, 9,
17, 19, 23

Printed in the U.S.A. - BG